Deserts

Neil Morris

CRABTREE PUBLISHING COMPANY

The Wonders of our World

Crabtree Publishing Company

350 Fifth Avenue, Suite 3308 New York, New York 10118	360 York Road, R. R. 4 Niagara-on-the-Lake, Ontario Canada L0S 1J0	73 Lime Walk Headington, Oxford England OX3 7AD

Author: Neil Morris
Managing editor: Peter Sackett
Editors: Ting Morris & David Schimpky
Designer: Richard Rowan
Production manager: Graham Darlow
Picture research: Lis Sackett

Picture Credits:
Artists: Martin Camm, Wildlife Art
Maps: European Map Graphics Ltd
Photographs: Bruce Coleman 5 (top), 26. Colorific 24
(bottom). Robert Harding Picture Library 4, 8 (top), 10
(bottom),
13 (bottom), 14, 26 (bottom), 27 (bottom left), 28 (top).
Frank Lane 5 (bottom), 6 (bottom), 7 (bottom), 10 (top),
13 (top), 16 (top), 17 (top right), 18 (bottom), 19 (bottom left),
23 (top), 29 (bottom). Silvestris 7 (top right). Topham
Picturepoint 3, 7 (top left), 8 (bottom), 9 (top), 16 (bottom),

Cataloging-in-publication data

Morris, Neil
    Deserts

(Wonders of our world)
Includes index.
ISBN 0-86505-827-X (library bound) ISBN 0-86505-839-3 (pbk.)
This book looks at the various aspects of deserts, including
natural features, wildlife, and the effect of humans.

1. Deserts - Juvenile literature. 2. Desert ecology - Juvenile
literature. I. Title. II. Series: Morris, Neil. Wonders of our
world.

GB612.M66 1995   j574.5'2652   LC 95-23440

CONTENTS

WHAT IS A DESERT?

A DESERT is an area of land where very little or no precipitation, such as rain or snow, falls. This lack of moisture means that the ground is totally dry nearly all the time.

We usually think of deserts as hot, sandy places like the Sahara Desert in Africa, but there are other desert landscapes. Any region that gets less than 25 centimeters (10 inches) of precipitation a year is called a desert. Deserts can be cold places, such as the Gobi Desert in Asia or the icy continent of Antarctica.

COASTAL DESERT

Desert areas near the sea get some moisture from fog. Less than 2.5 centimeters (1 inch) of rain falls each year in the Namib Desert (right), on the southwest coast of Africa. On many days, however, fog rolls in from the sea. This fog is caused by cold ocean currents cooling the warm air. The Atacama Desert in Chile is a similar coastal desert.

DRY, BARREN MOUNTAINS

As well as endless spaces filled with sand dunes, the Sahara Desert contains areas of rocks and mountains. The Ahaggar Mountains, in Algeria, rise to a height of nearly 3000 meters (9845 feet). This rocky region, surrounded by desert, was created long ago by erupting volcanoes. When the lava cooled, it formed these dramatic shapes.

DESERT ROCK AND SAND

The sand and dusty soil of deserts were once rock. Over thousands of years, rock is worn down into tiny particles. The "desert rose" is made of mineral crystals that are formed in sand dunes.

Fine sand

Coarse sand

Dust

Granite

Sandstone

Wind-blasted stone

Desert rose

Basalt

SNOW IN THE DESERT

SNOW SOMETIMES falls in the cooler deserts of the world. In the winter, light snow sometimes dusts the badlands of South Dakota, for example. Even hot deserts can become extremely cold at night, and frost can occur in winter. Snow seldom falls in the polar regions, although snow and ice permanently cover the ground. These areas are sometimes called ice deserts.

WHERE IN THE WORLD?

THE MAIN hot deserts are found in two bands that stretch around the world. One band of deserts is above the equator and straddles the Tropic of Cancer. It includes the Sahara and Arabian Deserts.

The other band, below the equator, runs along the Tropic of Capricorn. It includes the Atacama Desert in South America and the Great Sandy Desert of Australia.

Cold deserts, such as the Turkestan Desert and the Patagonian Desert, occur above or below these bands.

GOBI

The Gobi Desert, in Mongolia and China, is situated on a plateau that is up to 1500 meters (4920 feet) high. Some parts are rocky, while others have sand dunes.

THE WORLD'S DESERTS

Many hot deserts lie along the imaginary lines of the tropics, above and below the middle line of the equator.

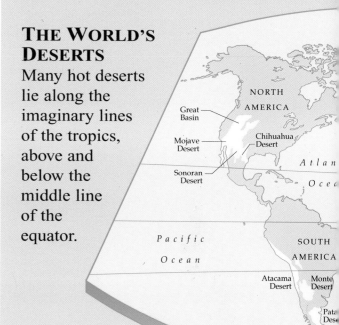

NORTH AMERICA

Great Basin

Mojave Desert

Chihuahua Desert

Sonoran Desert

Atlan

Ocea

Pacific Ocean

SOUTH AMERICA

Atacama Desert

Monte Desert

Pata Dese

SONORAN

THE Sonoran Desert, in the southwestern United States and northern Mexico, has 300 different types of cactus. It is also home to a variety of rare desert animals.

On the map:

GREENLAND

EUROPE

ASIA

Turkestan Desert

Gobi Desert

Iranian Desert

Takla Makan Desert

Thar Desert

Sahara Desert

Arabian Desert

AFRICA

Somali-Chalbi Desert

TROPIC OF CANCER

EQUATOR

Indian Ocean

Namib Desert

Great Sandy Desert

Simpson Desert

Kalahari Desert

Gibson Desert

TROPIC OF CAPRICORN

AUSTRALIA

Great Victoria Desert

GREAT VICTORIA
The Great Victoria Desert is the most southern of the four deserts that cover central Australia.

KALAHARI
Dry riverbeds run across the Kalahari Desert in southern Africa. This desert lies on the Tropic of Capricorn.

PATAGONIA
The Patagonian Desert of Chile and Argentina lies on a dry plateau that rises to the Andes Mountains. It reaches almost to the tip of South America.

THE SAHARA

THE SAHARA is the world's largest desert. It stretches across northern Africa, covering an area of about 9 million square kilometers (3.5 million square miles).

Huge areas of shifting sand dunes, called ergs, cover only about one-fifth of the Sahara. Most of the region is made up of rocky uplands called hamadas and flat stony plains called regs.

The Sahara is a very hot desert. In summer, temperatures can reach 50°C (122°F).

ROUNDED ROCKS

IN THE Sahara, as in all deserts, rocks are blasted by winds and wind-blown sand. Over centuries, the weathering has smoothed rocks that were once rough and craggy.

SANDSTONE PINNACLES

Ancient rock carvings and paintings have been found in the Sahara. They show that the region was once fertile and green. Ravines that once held rushing rivers were eroded by wind and sand until they became pinnacles.

SHIFTING SAND

IN PARTS of the Sahara, the only landmarks are sand dunes. Nothing here is permanent. The dunes move and drift, and a footprint can vanish in just a few hours.

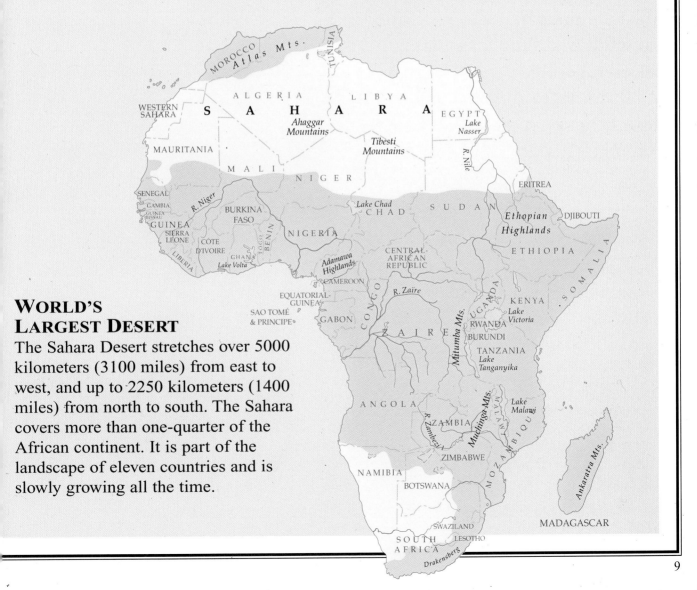

WORLD'S LARGEST DESERT

The Sahara Desert stretches over 5000 kilometers (3100 miles) from east to west, and up to 2250 kilometers (1400 miles) from north to south. The Sahara covers more than one-quarter of the African continent. It is part of the landscape of eleven countries and is slowly growing all the time.

9

SEAS OF SAND

THE LARGEST sandy region in the world is in southern Saudi Arabia. This part of the Arabian Desert is called Rub' al Khali, which means "Empty Quarter." The area is so hot and dry that it is one of the least-explored regions in the world.

A desert's sand forms over millions of years as rock crumbles. Driven by winds, the sand collects in the corner of a desert, or it forms dunes that cover huge areas like the Empty Quarter.

ON THE MOVE
Large sand dunes, like these in the Sahara Desert, sometimes travel up to 18 meters (60 feet) a year.

WIND ACTION
Like waves on the sea, sand dunes are shaped by the wind. Dunes move too, but much more slowly.

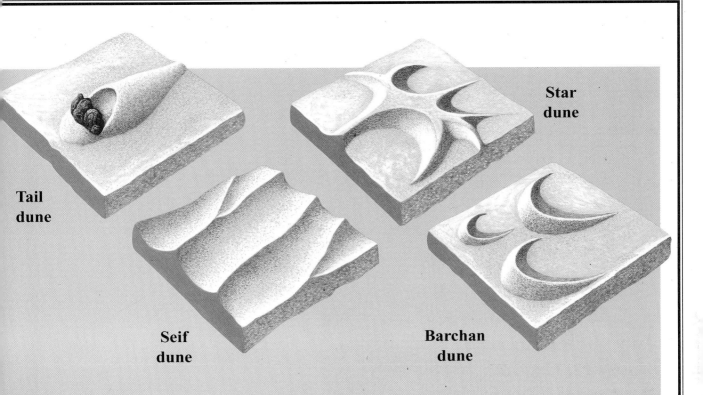

Tail
dune

Seif
dune

Star
dune

Barchan
dune

SAND DUNES

Dunes can have
many different
shapes, depending
mainly on the
wind. A tail dune
forms behind an
obstacle such as
a rock or a small
bush. Seifs are
long ridges that
can stretch over
great distances.
Star dunes form
when winds blow
from different
directions. Finally,
crescent-shaped
barchans often
form around a
boulder.

HOW DUNES FORM

A SAND dune
usually
forms around an
obstacle such as a
plant or rock. The
obstacle slows the
wind down and
makes it drop any
sand it is carrying.
The mound that
builds up acts as a
bigger barrier to
the wind. The crest
of the dune may
eventually collapse
like a wave.

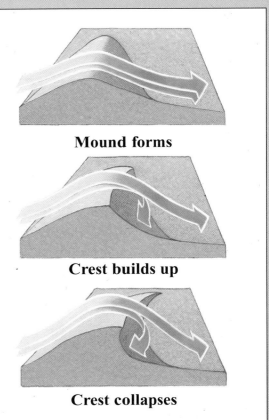

Mound forms

Crest builds up

Crest collapses

ROCKY WILDERNESS

OVER MILLIONS of years, rocks on the surface of the earth have been weathered. In other words, they have been worn away by the effects of heat, cold, water, and wind.

The world's hottest and driest places are rocky deserts. In California's scorching Death Valley, the temperature often rises to 43°C (110°F). In Chile's dry Atacama Desert, less than 0.1 millimeters (0.004 inches) of rain falls each year.

STONY DESERT

PARTS of the Atacama Desert are covered in stones. Long ago, this desert was covered by lakes and streams. Today, however, the Atacama Desert is one of the driest places on earth. It receives almost no precipitation.

DEVIL'S GOLF COURSE

IN Death Valley, sudden rainstorms sometimes cause floods that create a temporary lake called a playa. When the playa dries out, the salts from the water form a white layer on the flat valley floor. These salt flats are known as the Devil's Golf Course.

WEATHERED SPIRES

Scientists can study millions of years of the earth's history in the rocks of Bryce Canyon, in Utah. This canyon is near the edge of the Great Basin desert region. Its amazing landscape, including these spires, was formed by the effects of weathering.

HOT, DRY, AND LOW

California's Death Valley is the hottest, driest, and lowest place in North America. At one point, it is 86 meters (280 feet) below sea level. The valley is dry because moist winds from the Pacific Ocean drop their rain on coastal mountains. Much of Death Valley is barren rock, but sand sometimes collects in dunes.

ICY DESERTS

THE TWO polar regions of the earth are considered deserts because they receive little precipitation. The Arctic region, around the North Pole, is not as cold as Antarctica, the continent at the South Pole.

At the top and bottom of the world, winters are long and dark, and the temperatures are very low. The ground is frozen for most of the year, and soil thaws only at the surface. Water never sinks into the earth.

BREAKING AWAY

The ice around both polar regions grows larger in the winter and shrinks in the summer. Massive icebergs break away from the end of ice sheets or glaciers. Some are as big as small towns. Most of an iceberg is beneath the sea, so usually we see just the tip poking above the surface.

COLDEST CONTINENT

In winter, Antarctica is the coldest and windiest place on earth. Winters here last from May to September. The average temperatures can dip as low as -58ºC (-72ºF), and strong gales can blow at speeds of up to 320 kilometers per hour (200 miles per hour).

KINGS OF THE COLD

SEVERAL species of penguins and seals live in Antarctica and on nearby islands. These animals have a thick layer of blubber under their skin to help keep in body heat. Blubber also provides energy when food is scarce.

King penguins

Fur seal

DESERT PLANTS

SINCE ALL plants need water, few can survive in the desert. Some desert plants have long roots to get water from deep in the ground. Others store water in their roots, leaves, or stems. They have thick bark and waxy leaves to help them save water.

Some desert plants have very short lives. When it rains, seeds suddenly send up shoots. They flower within a few weeks, scattering new seeds before they die. The process begins again when it next rains —which may not be for years.

STORING WATER

The kokerboom tree grows in the deserts of southwestern Africa. It stores water in its trunk. This water storage method helps the tree survive without rain.

GIANT CACTI

THE SAGUARO cactus grows only in the Sonoran Desert. It has been known to grow to a height of over 17 meters (56 feet), making it the tallest of all cacti. Shallow roots spread out to gather moisture before water sinks far into the ground. Like all cacti, saguaros store water in their fleshy stems. Sharp spines protect these plants from hungry animals.

WATER!

A N OASIS is a small area with water in the desert. The water comes to the surface from porous rock. The water may rise due to a fault in layers of rock or a basin of land having been worn away. If desert dwellers know where water is, they can dig a well to make an oasis.

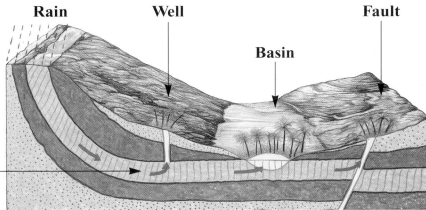

Rain   **Well**   **Fault**

Basin

Water in porous rock

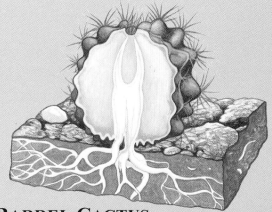

PRICKLY FLOWERS

The hedgehog cactus received its name because it has long, sharp spines. It grows about 15 centimeters (6 inches) high and has bright red flowers after rain. These cacti grow in North American deserts.

BARREL CACTUS

The barrel cactus's roots spread out to catch as much water as possible. Inside the cactus, beneath a thick waxy outer layer, is a mass of tissues that store the collected water.

INSECTS AND REPTILES

MANY INSECTS adapt well to life in the desert. Some have bodies enclosed in tough outer shells coated with wax. They can creep into tiny cracks in rocks for shelter from the heat.

Reptiles, such as snakes and lizards, are cold-blooded. They need heat from the sun to warm their bodies. Desert reptiles usually move about just after sunrise and before sunset, when the ground is warm. Their scaly skin stops them from losing too much water.

DESERT TORTOISE
This tortoise lives in the deserts of Mexico and the United States. During the hottest time of the day, it shelters in a burrow in the ground. It comes out later to feed on desert plants.

POISONOUS LIZARD

THE gila monster is a poisonous lizard that lives in the Mojave and Sonoran Deserts. The gila stores fat in its thick tail for use when there is a food shortage. This lizard can be up to 60 centimeters (24 inches) long.

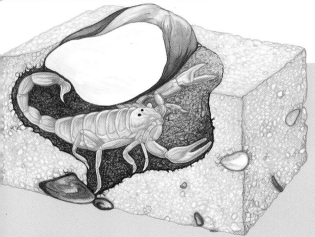

SCORPIONS

Different kinds of scorpions live in deserts all over the world. Like spiders, scorpions are arachnids—they have eight legs. They use their powerful stinger to kill prey.

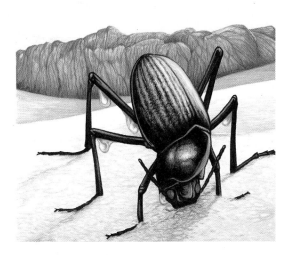

WATER AND FOOD

IN COASTAL deserts, the darkling beetle (above) lets moisture from fog collect on its body. The water droplets run down to its mouth. The larvae of ant lions (below) catch insects by building a sand trap. Adult ant lions look like dragonflies.

RATTLER

Rattlesnakes, like this diamondback, warn enemies away by rattling the loose rings of skin at the end of their tail. This is a better warning than hissing, which uses up water.

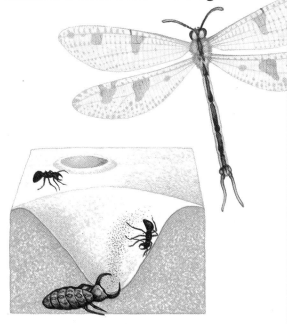

MAMMALS AND BIRDS

MOST DESERT mammals are small and live in burrows or under rocks during the day. They come out to feed at night. Larger desert animals, such as the gazelles and antelopes that live in the Sahara Desert, rest in sheltered areas in the heat of the day.

Birds cope well with desert conditions. They can fly in search of water, and their feathers help protect them from the burning sun.

LONG-EARED FOX

The fennec is the smallest fox, yet it is also the one with the longest ears. It lives in the Sahara and Arabian Deserts and uses its large ears to cool its body quickly. It has very good hearing, too!

BIRD OF PREY

THE Harris's hawk lives in the deserts and grasslands of North and South America. It swoops down and catches small animals such as rabbits and lizards. Meat-eating birds do not need to drink water, since they get moisture from their prey.

ROADRUNNER

The roadrunner lives in the deserts of the United States and Mexico. It rarely flies. Instead, when threatened, the roadrunner runs away at great speed. This bird also chases anything that moves.

CACTUS NESTS

THE gila woodpecker (far right) pecks its way into a giant saguaro cactus to make its nest. The tiny elf owl (right) waits its turn and nests in the woodpecker's hole when it has been abandoned.

LONG JUMPER

Red kangaroos live in the Australian outback. They jump along on their powerful back legs, using their tail for balance. They can leap up to 9 meters (30 feet) in one huge bound.

HOPPING RAT

The kangaroo rat nests in a burrow during the day. It gets its name from its long back legs, on which it hops along in search of seeds to eat.

SHIP OF THE DESERT

CAMELS ARE large, strong animals that are very well suited to life in the desert. They can go without food and water for days at a time. Fat, stored in their humps, provides them with energy. As the camel slowly burns up fat, the hump shrinks.

Long lashes and thick brows help to protect the camel's eyes from the sun and sand. A camel can also quickly shut its nostrils into slits when there is a sandstorm.

MOUNTING A CAMEL
A camel tucks its legs under its body when it rests on the ground. Tough pads on its knees and chest allow the camel to kneel comfortably. Riders mount when the camel is sitting down.

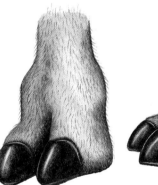

FOOT PADS
Camels have broad foot pads, which help them walk on soft sand without sinking. Each foot has two toes and a very tough sole.

DROMEDARY

The one-humped Arabian camel is called a dromedary. It lives in the deserts of North Africa, the Arabian Peninsula, and Asia. People use the dromedary to carry loads. It is often called the "ship of the desert." Camels also provide meat, milk, and fleece for desert peoples.

BACTRIAN CAMEL

BACTRIAN CAMELS have two humps on their backs. They are found in the deserts of central Asia. Here winters are cold, and the ground is sometimes covered in snow. The Bactrian camel has a long, woolly coat, with longer hair on its throat, shoulders, and humps to keep it warm.

The rider holds on tight as the camel stands up. First, it gets into a kneeling position, then pushes its back legs up before standing on its front legs. Camels are good pack animals and can carry as much as 270 kilograms (600 pounds).

PEOPLE OF THE DESERT

FEWER PEOPLE live in deserts than in other parts of the world. Certain peoples, however, have adapted well to desert life.

Nomads travel the desert, moving from one oasis to another. They use camels and donkeys to carry their tents and possessions.

The San people of the Kalahari Desert and the Aborigines of Australia are hunter-gatherers. They eat plants and roots gathered by the women, and small animals hunted by the men.

FIRST AUSTRALIANS
The Aborigines went to Australia from Asia around 40,000 years ago. They learned to survive in the desert. Many Aborigines continue to follow the traditional ways of their people.

THE SAN

THE San people, or Bushmen, of the Kalahari get water by sucking it through hollow reeds stuck in the ground. They are skilled hunters, using arrows tipped with poison made from beetles.

THE BEDOUIN

THE NOMADIC Bedouin people of Arabia and the Sahara rear camels and sell them at markets in oasis towns.

Traditional Bedouin travel the deserts with their camels and herds of goats and sheep. Bedouin family groups live in tents made of goat's hair that are easy to put up and take down.

THE INUIT

The Inuit live in the frozen wilderness of the Arctic. In the past, Inuit hunters traveled the icy landscape on sleds. They used kayaks to catch fish, seals, and even whales. A small number still live in this way, but many Inuit now live in larger settlements.

MONGOLS

Mongolian nomads live in camps of round felt tents called yurts. The felt is made of sheep's wool. Mongols move about in search of pasture for their sheep and horses. Some tribes keep oxen and camels.

MINERAL WEALTH

VALUABLE minerals are found in the world's deserts. Oil is one of the most important riches in the desert. Its discovery brought great wealth to the countries of the Middle East. The icy desert of the Arctic is another area where oil and natural gas are found.

Gold, silver, and diamonds are also mined beneath the surface of hot deserts. Mining and other enterprises, however, can endanger desert plants and animals by using up scarce sources of water.

DESERT DIAMONDS

The Namib Desert, in southwest Africa, is a major source of diamonds. Mining is an important part of the economy of Namibia.

AUSTRALIAN GOLD

GOLD has been mined from the Australian deserts for about 150 years. Today, Australia is the fourth biggest producer of gold in the world, and is rich in other minerals as well.

ALASKAN PIPELINE

A huge pipeline carries oil from the frozen oilfields of northern Alaska to the port of Valdez. The pipeline was built above the frozen earth. Parts of the pipeline are raised high above the ground so caribou can pass underneath.

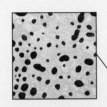

Dead sea plants and animals buried

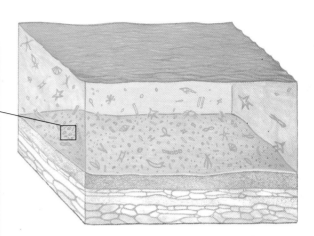

Millions of years ago

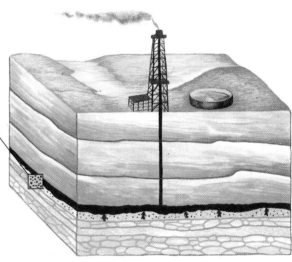

Oil collects in reservoir rocks

Today

HOW OIL FORMED

MILLIONS OF years ago, the remains of dead sea plants and animals were covered by mud and sand. Heat and pressure slowly turned the remains into oil, which was held between solid rocks. Many areas that were covered by sea millions of years ago are now desert. Wells bring oil from deep in the ground to the surface.

SPREADING DESERTS

MANY OF the world's deserts are growing. The process by which deserts spread is called desertification. Many deserts spread because fertile land on the borders of deserts is misused.

In these areas, people sometimes burn or cut down vegetation. Some farmers overwork the land or allow herds to graze pastures bare. When droughts occur, the wind blows the good soil away. We must use land more carefully if we are to stop desertification.

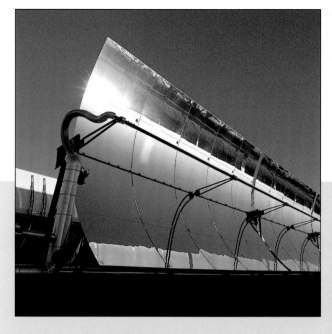

SOLAR ENERGY
Solar panels collect the sun's energy and turn it into electricity. Hot deserts like the Mojave are perfect places to collect solar energy because they are so sunny.

A LOST OASIS
An oasis can be lost if sand dunes move and bury it. The oasis may then be gone for many years—perhaps forever. Damage from wind and sand can be reduced or stopped by planting grasses. The roots hold the sand together to keep dunes in place.

Key
Existing Desert
High Risk Area
Medium Risk Area

Pacific Ocean

Atlantic Ocean

Indian Ocean

AREAS AT RISK

This world map shows the areas most at risk from the spread of deserts. These high-risk areas are usually around the edges of existing deserts.

The biggest desert of all, the Sahara, could spread both to the north and south. Large areas of central Asia, Australia, and the western United States are also in danger of desertification.

OVERGRAZING

IF PEOPLE allow their animals to graze freely, desert plants soon disappear. This can help deserts spread. Overgrazing also takes food away from wild desert animals, who rely on the plants.

GLOSSARY

Arachnids   Small, eight-legged animals similar to insects. Spiders and scorpions are arachnids.

Bactrian   The two-humped Asian camel.

Barchan   Describes a crescent-shaped sand dune.

Bark   The outer, protective layer of a plant.

Basin   A depression in the earth's surface.

Blubber   A thick layer of fat under an animal's skin.

Continent   One of the earth's seven huge land masses.

Desertification   The process by which fertile land becomes desert.

Dromedary   The one-humped Arabian camel.

Drought   A long period of very little rainfall.

Dune   A mound of sand.

Equator   An imaginary circle that stretches around the middle of the earth.

Erg   An area of shifting sand dunes.

Fault   A fracture in the earth's surface.

Hamada   A raised area of rocky land.

Iceberg   A large mass of ice floating in the sea.

Ice cap   A thick mass of ice that covers an area of land.

Kayak   A canoe-like boat with a light covered frame.

Larva   The young stage of many insects.

Mammals	Warm-blooded animals, such as cats, mice, bats, and monkeys, that feed their young with milk.
Mineral	A substance that occurs naturally in the earth.
Nomad	A person who wanders from place to place to find grazing land and food.
Oasis	An area in a desert with water, where plants can grow.
Outback	The bush country of Australia, where very few people live.
Plain	Flat countryside with few trees.
Plateau	A flat area of high land.
Playa	A temporary lake in a desert basin.
Polar	Near one of the earth's two poles, the North Pole or the South Pole.
Porous	Describes something that lets water through.
Reg	A flat stony plain.
Reptiles	Cold-blooded, usually scaly animals, including tortoises, snakes, and lizards.
Seif dune	A long ridge of blown sand.
Species	One variety of animal.
Tropic	One of the two imaginary lines that stretch around the earth near the equator; the Tropic of Cancer is above the equator, and the Tropic of Capricorn is below it.
Weather	To wear (rocks) away by the effects of the weather.
Yurt	A round tent made of felt.

INDEX

123456789 Printed in the U.S.A. 432109876